TAX TIME
TALES
'Tinis & Toddies

Book design by:
Arbor Services, Inc.
www.arborservices.co/

Printed in the United States of America

Tax Time Tales - 'Tinis & Toddies
Michael Carminucci

1. Title 2. Author 3. Humor

Library of Congress Control Number: 2018906753
ISBN 13: 978-0-692-13585-3

TAX TIME TALES
'Tinis & Toddies

MICHAEL CARMINUCCI

Carminucci Wealth Management

*Dedicated to the Internal Revenue Service
who inspired me to write this book, making it an absolute
necessity at tax time.*

Contents

Introduction

Well, it's tax season again, at least at the time of this book's composition, and if you're not much of a drinker most months of the year, people will excuse you for being one now. The combination of losing money, interacting with the government, completing endless paperwork, and shivering through cold weather is enough to justify picking up the habit for a few days, weeks, or months. If you already indulge on a regular basis, carry on.

Taxes and alcohol have a rich history together. In 1791, an extra charge on whiskey became the first tax imposed on a domestically produced product. Not surprisingly, this was a very unpopular move by the newly formed US government, and maybe a bad choice given their circumstances. George Washington's administration needed money, so more taxes were inevitable. Unfortunately, the feds had just made the substance most capable of helping people forget about government hands dipping into their pockets, harder to get.

This tax led to the Whiskey Rebellion, the first major violent protest in United States history. Though not the nation's proudest moment, it proclaimed the importance of two things: our revolutionary ideals and our booze. While each has found a different place in the national culture over the years, they have never stopped being major parts of this country's identity.

Two hundred odd years later, the government now taxes nearly everything—our income, our property, and yes, every kind of alcohol available; all are taxed. This would be a tough idea for many revolutionary-era Americans to grasp. Although, thanks to taxes, we now have the air force, among other things, so maybe the benefits have evened out a little.

Regardless of any justifications for government money, tax time will never be an enjoyable time of year for most Americans. The tax code is arcane and impossible to decipher. The government is a bureaucratic mess that no person can navigate without practically tearing their hair out. And if you are responsible for a company and not only personal finances, you may need hours of therapy following this ordeal.

Perhaps worst of all, you can never predict how long the process will take. That's where this book comes in. The only way to get through tax season is with a drink in your hand occasionally—if not always. A little buzz helps the government-mandated shellacking go down a little easier. So, head to a nearby liquor store, grab a bottle of Jack Daniel's finest and some Coke, and tip a few back. To keep your sanity, there's no other option.

"Our new Constitution is now established and has an appearance that promises permanency; but in this world, nothing can be said to be permanent, except death and taxes." *–Benjamin Franklin*

"The only difference between death and taxes is that death doesn't get worse every time Congress meets." *–Will Rogers*

Part 1:
Beginning with the Basics: Mixed Drinks

Our version of the EZ-Form: If you don't want to exert yourself too much or use a barrage of ingredients, following are some simple concoctions to start with. Simply combine some soda or juice with the right kind of booze, and you'll end up with an easy kick to take the edge off.

ACCOUNTANTS
AND
AUDITORS

a. bacall

"Now, using a little accounting magic on your tax return, one and one equals three."

CartoonStock.com

Screwed by the Government Screwdriver

Quick and simple, it won't take long for you to feel this citrus blend boring down. Take these slow or you'll be in for a rough morning; the same goes for filing your taxes.

Ingredients:

5 oz. orange juice

2 oz. New Amsterdam original vodka

Pinch of salt

1 rusty screwdriver

Mixing Instructions:

Pour orange juice into a glass, then gradually add the vodka. Sprinkle in a pinch of salt for good measure. Stir with a rusty screwdriver. If no screwdriver is available, a rusty nail will do (really any aging, tarnished tool will do: hammer, monkey wrench, etc.). When the feds come knocking down the door, you can buy some time with a trip to the hospital to recover from tetanus.

Any vodka works as a substitute for New Amsterdam. In the absence of vodka, substitute anything from moonshine to mouthwash. The orange juice is best if fresh squeezed. When that's not an option, make sure to at least cut down on pulp. The thickness of pulpy orange juice does not pair with vodka (or mouthwash) or any drink that's not well blended. Grapefruit juice is also a workable substitute for orange juice. Tanginess will cut through the bite of the vodka a little more.

- Thanks to a Florida tax credit for farmers, many of whom supply the oranges that provide the juice for your screwdrivers, renting cows is a bustling business. Savvy developers, including Walt Disney years ago, found they could qualify for this credit by hosting a few heifers on their land. While this practice might go against the original spirit of the tax credit, no one can fault these "faux farmers" for creativity.

- Actor Wesley Snipes neglected to pay taxes from 1999 to 2004. When confronted by the IRS, he claimed he was a resident alien, despite listing his birth place simply as "Florida." He may have had a few too many screwdrivers before making this argument.

Docile Dependent

This drink WORKS ONLY when made by a dependent (no one else's kid will do). Since most dependents are on the young side, we wanted to suggest something that is easy enough for a six-year-old to make. Its simplicity makes for quick mixing, and the potency of the rum is offset just enough by the Coke and lime.

Ingredients:

1 oz. Captain Morgan rum—black

3 oz. Coca-Cola

2 lime lollypops (one for the drink and one for the dependent)

Mixing Instructions:

Pour one ounce of rum into a glass with some ice. Slowly add an equal amount of the Coke. Stir vigorously with lollypop.

For variation, grind up a Tootsie Pop and sprinkle the shards in. Some may prefer different sodas; go for it! Substitute Sprite, root beer, grape soda, or lose the soda altogether and add more lollypops (one for each dependent you carry!)

"We contend that a nation trying to tax itself into prosperity is like a man standing in a bucket trying to pick himself up by the handle." *–Winston Churchill*

- In 2016, the IRS allowed a business to deduct gifts of beer to clients as a business expense but declined to do the same for whiskey and rum. It looks like the recent "Beer Revolution" we're all witnessing is backed by government agents. Liquor producers everywhere should take note.

- Hawaii residents can deduct $3,000 from their taxes for "the care of an exceptional tree." To prevent people from claiming a five-foot sapling as a dependent, the IRS sends "tree experts" to evaluate whether the tree is exceptional. This arboreal audit has no doubt made for some strange conversations.

Tax Bracket

Perhaps people connect part of their identity with their income and therefore their tax bracket. As it has only a little mixer, the Tax Bracket is a kick in the teeth, and so something of a personality test in its own way. At least you'll know more about your "liquor palette" after trying this.

Ingredients:

2 oz. dry gin

2 oz. Rumple Minze

2 oz. Sprite

1 slice lime

Mixing Instructions:

Combine the gin, Rumple Minze, and Sprite in a highball—6- to 8-ounce glass. Garnish with a lime slice on the edge of the glass.

Don't take this potent mixer down too quickly. The Tax Bracket is for sipping on a relaxing evening so you have a level head the next morning. No one wants to take on tax day with a hangover. Drinking more than one of these is not for the faint of heart.

"A fine is a tax for doing something wrong. A tax is a fine for doing something right." *–Anonymous*

- In Pennsylvania, there is literally a tax on having fun. Known as the "amusement tax," the state adds a 5% sales tax to movie or concert tickets, bowling shoe rental, and any number of sports-related activities.

- Five-time Grammy award winner Lauryn Hill couldn't sing her way out of tax problems. Despite having sold over eight million records, she ended up doing three months for neglecting to fork over roughly a million dollars in taxes.

- In Chicago, certain candies are favored above others. If a candy has flour in it, it is taxed 5.5% less than candies without. When you are in the area, stock up on Kit Kat bars and licorice.

Beachfront Property Deduction Blitz

Have you been claiming thousands of dollars a year as a deduction for your one-time boat rental on Lake George? Maybe it is time to head south of the border. You might want to wear some sunglasses while drinking this; it's the right mix to take with you while you're trying to beat the heat of the Mexican sun.

Ingredients:

2 oz. Patrón Silver tequila

½ oz. lime juice

7 oz. grapefruit Jarritos

Mixing Instructions:

Combine the tequila and lime juice in a glass. Pour the Jarritos on top. For a stronger drink, use less soda. Five ounces of soda, and the drink will be about as potent as a glass of wine. Four or three ounces, and you are in margarita territory. Anything below that is really going to blow your hair back.

If you are not familiar, Jarritos is a common Mexican soda that is usually not hard to find. However, there are numerous American alternatives, such as IZZE and Fresca, that taste just fine. Of course, you can experiment with different flavored sodas. It's a good idea to stick with fruit; pomegranate or pineapple make for an interesting variation.

- In New Jersey, a man successfully deducted a new below-ground pool from his tax expenses, claiming a doctor insisted on daily swimming to maintain his health. Swimming is a great weight loss tactic, so maybe this surprising deduction is a solid excuse to put on a few pounds.

- Hollywood Madam Heidi Fleiss was arrested and served prison time when a man at the IRS found she hadn't been reporting all her earnings. The money was flowing in from her bustling Los Angeles brothel, which supposedly saw many superstar clients. How the IRS agent became intimately aware of Ms. Fleiss's business is still a mystery.

- Taxes never die in Alabama. Despite the last veterans of the Civil War being dead for over sixty years, Alabamans are paying yearly taxes to fund the Alabama Confederate Soldiers Home. The money has long been repurposed for other needs, but the tax remains in effect.

- Seven states have no income tax: Alaska, Florida, Nevada, South Dakota, Texas, Washington, and Wyoming. If you are considering moving to save a little dough, you should be aware that each state has found a way to make up for that lack of revenue, including massively expanding income and property taxes. Uncle Sam is always going to have his due.

- Martin Scorsese has a history of not paying his fair share of taxes on time. Twice, the IRS has taken over some of Scorsese's properties until he paid up an estimated $3 million.

- Lottery winners almost always have trouble with the IRS. The federal government keeps a close eye on people who suddenly come into vast sums of money, and state governments take their due as well. Only California, Florida, New Hampshire, Pennsylvania, South Dakota, Washington, and Wyoming don't grab their share. There is a catch: if you manage to win the lottery while in Puerto Rico, no government agency will take a nickel.

Bankruptcy Bulleit Bourbon Cocktail

If the IRS has done their work and your bank account hits zero, this drink is perfect. A personal Black Tuesday requires an occasion-specific drink, and the Bankruptcy Bulleit Cocktail is just that.

Ingredients:

4 oz. Bulleit Kentucky bourbon

1 oz. tonic water

1 oz. Coca-Cola

1 bullet

Mixing Instructions:

Combine bourbon, tonic water, and Coke in a rocks glass. To properly consume, drop a bullet into the concoction and down in one go. Finishing the Bankruptcy Cocktail isn't easy, but neither is bankruptcy. For extra punch, grab some pliers, pry open the bullet, and stir in the gunpowder.

- Certain towns have gone to extreme lengths to avoid paying high taxes. In 1909, Ulysses, Kansas, moved their entire city, buildings included, to circumvent newly raised property taxes on their old land. The town was successful, but only temporarily, as the state government caught on to their scheme the next year.

- Some states are more nostalgic for bygone eras than others. Texas supports residents who want to live like it's the Ol' West. All cowboy boots are exempt from state taxes. The same cannot be said for cowboys, unfortunately.

- A recent poll showed that, on average, Americans believe NASA's budget for space exploration accounts for 20% of annual spending. In 2016, NASA got about .005% of the total federal allowance.

Standard Deduction

A staple of any definitive drinking reference, the Standard Deduction is simple, but if given enough attention, it can wow any drinker.

Ingredients:

2 oz. Tanqueray dry gin

2 lime wedges

4½ oz. tonic water

Mixing Instructions:

Pour the gin into a chilled glass. Add three large ice cubes. Be careful not to chip when dropping. Squeeze in one lime wedge. Add the tonic water. Squeeze in a second lime wedge, then spear it on the rim of the glass.

This recipe is straightforward, but it can take a lot of tweaking to get just right. The correct ratio of tonic water to gin can vary slightly based on the gin's proof, origin, and quality. It's easy to mess up and get a drink that tastes like a watered-down shot, so take your time. For a lighter variation, use a gin with less juniper, such as Plymouth or Hendrick's.

- Missouri has installed a financial incentive for men to get married. The Show-Me State adds a $1 tax every year for unmarried men between the ages of twenty-one and fifty. Such a small amount of money is not a huge motivator, but it has been on the books since 1820. Taxing bachelors for almost two hundred years has generated millions of dollars for Missouri.

- In New York, the father of an aspiring Motocross racer spent over $160,000 in motorcycle equipment for his son. To offset the cost, he made his real estate company his son's sponsor, and the IRS allowed him to write off every penny of the $160,000 as a business expense come tax season.

Reasonable Refund

Another classic when mixed right, this unassuming tincture is a brilliant addition to your repertoire. Just like a regular little refund, some more casual participants prefer this to the toil and trouble of more extravagant attempts to get drunk/make money.

Ingredients:

1 ½ oz. vodka

4 oz. cranberry juice

1 lime wedge

Mixing Instructions:

Pour vodka into a highball glass. Slowly add the cranberry juice, stirring the whole time. Garnish with lime wedge.

While high-quality vodka will, of course, make for a better drink, don't feel like you need to overspend to make a good "reasonable refund"; any brand will do. People who prefer tequila should swap the vodka for two ounces of Jose Cuervo or Patrón Blanco tequila; the fruit blend is fantastic. Variations on juices are also common; substitute one ounce of the cranberry juice for an ounce of orange or even pineapple juice.

"Other people's films are like a cocktail, a little alcohol mixed with water and juice. My films are like pure vodka." *–Jiang Wen*

- William Abbot and Lou Costello weren't as precise with their finances as they were with their wording in the witty bit "Who's on First" that made them famous. The comic duo split after selling the rights to almost all their material to pay the IRS for back taxes. Apparently "who" was the US government all along.

- Minnesota is known as one of the coldest states in the country but not as a hot spot for fashion. Regardless, their state government is particular about how their citizens stay warm and in vogue. The state government adds an 8% tax on coats made from real animal fur. However, this charge does not apply to similar coats if the fur is fake.

- People working out of a home office can deduct the cost of lawn and bush maintenance. All yard tools, such as mowers or hedge clippers, can be listed as a business expense. Technically you're keeping your work building looking presentable to clients and colleagues.

"I got 2 years for filing false returns, but I did save a bundle by doing my own taxes."

- Septic systems are an essential part of any healthy domestic situation, and Maryland is taking advantage of that necessity. One of Maryland's natural treasures, Chesapeake Bay, is in desperate need of environmental cleanup. The state has instituted a $60 tax every year on households that have a septic system. Proceeds from that tax go to fixing and maintaining Chesapeake Bay.

- Chuck Berry, famed as a pioneer of rock music and the writer of "Johnny B. Good," had chronic tax problems. In 1979, the legendary musician spent 120 days in jail for tax evasion. The IRS specifically labelled him as a "chronic tax evader" in their written charges.

- Electronic tax returns are not only easier and quicker than paper returns, they're more likely to net you a refund. According to a Pew Research Center study, people who file on paper are forty-one times more likely to commit an error that leads to them overpaying compared to people who file electronically.

Early Filing

Just want to get this whole thing over with fast? An early filing and the Early Filing will do exactly that.

Ingredients:

3 oz. Campari liqueur

4 oz. pineapple juice

½ oz. lemon juice

½ oz. lime

4 green apple Jolly Ranchers

1 lemon slice

Mixing Instructions:

Slowly combine the Campari and juices in a highball glass. Drop in four Jolly Ranchers, two ice cubes, and garnish with a lemon slice.

This basic combination of Campari and juices is sweet, but the high ratio of Campari will cut right though the shaker. You can experiment with other liqueurs, including a sweet Dolin vermouth—just 2 oz.—or Cointreau. Different flavors of Jolly Rancher can create a wide range of flavor groupings. If you crush the candy before mixing it in, the taste will pop out to a much higher degree.

- A wine's aroma is a key aspect of its quality. The IRS is always more than ready to help pay for wine experts' operations to keep their sniffing abilities intact.

- Hunters who prefer a bow and arrow to a rifle need to be careful of their arrow length; the feds have stepped in. If arrows are eighteen inches or longer, they are subject to an excise tax of 46 cents per shaft. Shorter bolts are a little cheaper but require more skill.

- A California woman felt she needed consistent tanning, manicures, and even Botox to maintain her self-confidence while working. When she filed her taxes with these image enhancers attached as deductions, the taxman did not react favorably.

Flat Tax

A flat tax can be extremely beneficial for a corporation, and the Flat Tax can be extremely beneficial to you on the right day. When the IRS has got you down, whip up a quick one of these and you'll be back on your feet. There's not much of a taste except the snap of the liquor, but it does the job.

Ingredients:

1 oz. bourbon

1 oz. rum

2 oz. flat soda

Several sheets old newspaper or cardboard

Mixing Instructions:

Combine all ingredients in a highball glass. Stir together with a strip of cardboard. If desired, pepper in old shredded newspaper or wood shavings as a garnish. Do not blend; having bits of trash floating in this drink is part of the rustic charm.

The Flat Tax is boring. If you're having fun drinking it, you probably mixed it wrong. Part of the appeal of this concoction is its lack of interesting features. No ups and downs; what you see is what you get. When in doubt, forget about using a glass or soda. Just take pulls of bourbon and rum together, eat some newspaper, and let the drink mix in your mouth.

- If you are really against taxes, Alaska is the place to go. Alaska has no sales tax on any product, and income taxes are virtually nonexistent. The state makes most of its money from petroleum revenues. Thank the tax gods for gasoline.

- The US is far from the only country with some upsetting tax laws. For years, England taxed windows in houses. Legislators' goal was to target rich citizens who had big homes or could afford a lot of glass, which was expensive at the time.

- Leaving the country won't stop the IRS from taking their due. The US still taxes citizens living outside its borders. Taxmen will chase you from here until Timbuktu, and ultimately, you'll pay the price.

Part 2:

Picking Up the Pace: Expediting Cocktails

It's time to move up in complexity a little. Typically, crafting the perfect cocktail requires a few extra steps. These might require a shaker, crushed ice, and a longer list of ingredients—plus, of course, a fancy glass to sip it in. If you don't have access to a shaker, a water bottle is a reasonable substitute; just don't shake too hard.

Taxes? They're a penalty for doing well.

CartoonStock.com

Checkbook Checkup Ceremony

Throughout the year, make sure to stay in touch with your personal finances. You'll need to be ready when tax season comes. No one wants to be sorting through a pile of unrecognizable receipts and old checks from half a year ago. Drink a Checkbook Checkup to commemorate this monthly ritual.

Ingredients:

2 oz. rye whiskey

3 oz. blue mouthwash

3 maraschino cherries

8 cancelled checks

1 oz. green mouthwash

Mixing Instructions:

Combine whiskey and three ounces blue mouthwash in a glass. Drop in the cherries from five inches above the mixture. Rip the checks into eighths and toss them in the air so some pieces land in the drink and others in the surrounding area. Pour the remaining mouthwash in a shot glass. Down the first mixture in one go; make sure you drink some of the old check pieces. Immediately follow that drink up with the shot of green mouthwash.

If you follow these steps exactly, your monthly finances will not have any unpleasant surprises. If you make mistakes, five days later, you will discover a discrepancy that may cost you thousands of dollars.

Tax Shelter

A drink for the ages, once you try this definitive cocktail, it's sure to become a favorite. Just like a handy financial arrangement to dodge the grasp of the feds, once you start a Tax Shelter, you'll keep coming back.

Ingredients:

1 sugar cube

4 dashes Angostura bitters

1 thin orange slice

1 maraschino cherry

1 splash club soda

2 oz. Bulleit straight bourbon

Mixing Instructions:

In a highball glass, muddle the sugar, bitters, orange slice, and maraschino cherry. Remove the leftover orange rind and add a splash of club soda. Slowly pour in the bourbon while stirring. Add several ice cubes while being careful not to chip, and garnish with another orange slice, if desired.

If sugar cubes aren't available, then a teaspoon of granulated white sugar works. Jim Beam and Old Overholt are good low-budget bourbon options. Connoisseurs with a more sophisticated pallet may prefer Sazerac straight rye for its robust piquancy. Preferences vary when it comes to liquor levels in a Tax Shelter. If you feel like sipping slowly for a while, add a half ounce of bourbon.

- The Alabama state government wants its taxpayers to be ready for anything. Concerned citizens who build radioactive fallout shelters in their backyard to stay safe in case of a nuclear blast receive a $1,000 deduction. So, take note: in case of incoming Armageddon, head to Dixie.

- New Mexico rewards their citizens who live to one hundred years old. If you make it to the triple-digit club in our forty-seventh state, you are no longer required to pay New Mexico taxes. Unfortunately, the federal government still takes what they can get.

- Not all foods are governed by the same tax laws. New York City, a town with a reputation for good bagels, adds a 9% tax after they are cut. If you want to save a little cash in the Big Apple, buy your bagels whole and cut them yourself.

Extraordinary Exemption

Successfully claim your thirty-eight-year-old son as a dependent? Celebrate your slick evasion in style with something imaginative. The Extraordinary Exemption is exactly the drink for that.

Ingredients:

2 oz. gin
½ oz. Dolin Blanc vermouth
¼ oz. maraschino liquor
3 dashes orange bitters

Mixing Instructions:

Half fill a shaker with ice. Slowly add the gin, vermouth, and liquor; shake to mix. Don't shake too hard or the ice will chip. Strain out the ice, return the mixture to shaker, and add the bitters. Stir slowly until bitters are evenly distributed. Pour the drink into chilled cocktail glass.

The Extraordinary Exemption is a strong drink, so be prepared for kick. For something a bit sweeter, you can add liquor and lower an equal amount of gin. Don't go past ¾ ounces of the liquor or the mixture will be too syrupy. To save money on the vermouth, try Martini & Rossi or Noilly Prat. If you aren't a fan of bitters, a little orange juice might be more to your liking.

- Under federal law, criminals who do not report stolen property can be indicted for tax fraud as well as theft if they are caught. The only safe option is to report those assets under "other income" or to not steal things.

- A stylist in Missouri tried to write off a year's worth of clothes shopping with the explanation that she needed to look presentable while cutting hair, thus making her wardrobe a business expense. While she faced an extensive audit, the IRS eventually decided that the woman had a point and allowed the deduction to stand.

- Nevada is friendly to body oil companies. Las Vegas is home to many bodybuilding competitions, including the Mr. Olympia yearly world championship. To help its muscle-bound residents, Nevada lets professional strength athletes deduct the cost of body oil and tanning lotion as a business expense.

Loony Loophole

The Loony Loophole has a more elusive taste than some of the previous drinks. Most cocktails home in on a flavor profile, but you'll find each experience with this brew wholly unique.

Ingredients:

½ oz. lemon juice

½ oz. lime juice

½ tsp. white sugar

2 ½ oz. Jose Cuervo tequila

1 oz. Grand Marnier orange liqueur

Serve in a Bugs Bunny glass and garnish with a carrot

Splash of club soda

Mixing Instructions:

Combine lemon juice, lime juice, and sugar in a shaker. Slowly add tequila and orange liqueur. Add ice and mix well. Strain into a Bugs Bunny or Road Runner glass; garnish with carrot or birdseed. Splash club soda on top.

The Loony Loophole is not particularly strong. To make it a little more "loopy," add a ½ ounce tequila or forget about the club soda.

Don't tamper with the orange liqueur too much, as it can quickly overwhelm the other ingredients. Patrón and Grand Mayan tequila are solid choices here if you aren't a fan of Jose Cuervo.

" YOU DEDUCTED WHOOPIE CUSHIONS AS A BUSINESS EXPENSE . JUST WHAT KIND OF BUSINESS ARE YOU IN, MR. QUINCY ? "

Taxidermist

Although taxidermy has nothing to do with taxes, they are both similar in that you wind up being hollowed out and stuffed with sawdust. This drink will help to alleviate the pain involved.

Ingredients:
1 oz. of each item in your liquor cabinet
4 oz. grated wine cork
5 beer caps

Mixing Instructions:
Fill glass to the brim and stir gently with a scalpel. Mix in the wine cork and beer caps. Drink quickly to avoid the flavor.

If you feel like taxes are making you lose your marbles, think about adding some to the Taxidermist. Clean several marbles—preferably green ones—and soak them in gin. After about three weeks, add the gin-infused marbles to your Taxidermist. It's an interesting twist that will probably not change the taste whatsoever. Give it a try anyway.

"What is the difference between a taxidermist and a tax collector? The taxidermist takes only your skin." –*Mark Twain*

"And, of course, that one is my favorite trophy."

"MY MISTAKE WAS WRITING TO THE I.R.S. TO THANK THEM FOR NOT AUDITING ME THAT YEAR."

- The IRS has extremely specific rules about how much of a deduction you can receive for donating a taxidermy animal to a museum. As the market value for most taxidermy is virtually impossible to appraise, the deduction you can take is all based on how much work you did to procure and create the "presentation." Appraising taxidermy for the IRS? There's a niche.

- The South Carolina government does not like deer, but people there do seem to enjoy venison. Hunters in the Palmetto State can receive a $75 tax credit for every deer carcass they donate to charity. If the meat is fresh and safe to eat once cooked, South Carolinians can save on their taxes by indulging in a hobby.

- In 2016, the average person spent thirteen hours on their taxes, and the IRS combed through 152.25 million tax returns. That adds up to eighty-two million days' worth of people preparing tax forms in one year. If that is not staggering enough, IRS agents spent tens of thousands more days checking forms once they were filled out.

Sin Tax

The American tax system classifies several taxes as "sin taxes." These charges include various levies on things like tobacco and alcohol. It's only natural that there's a drink to go with these sins. The Sin Tax is perfect if you are looking to impress someone. This drink goes down best if you enjoy it in your finest lace negligee and stiletto heels (regardless of your gender).

Ingredients:

1 oz. Patrón XO cafe liqueur
1 ½ oz. Patrón reposado tequila
¾ oz. chocolate liqueur
Fresh whipped cream
Crushed red pepper, optional

Mixing Instructions:

Combine cafe liqueur, tequila, and chocolate liqueur in a shaker with ice. Shake well, and strain mixture into a chilled highball glass. Top with a little whipped cream. Sprinkle crushed red pepper on top for a nice contrast to bring out the sweetness of the liqueurs.

Patrón is, of course, not the only option for tequila, although stick to reposado if you can. The other two varieties of tequila, blanco and añejo, won't pair as well. Blancos have a tanginess that clashes with the café and chocolate liqueurs. Añejos are far too strong, and their natural woodiness might overwhelm the cocktail.

- The IRS is encouraging people to quit smoking. Products specifically made to help Americans kick recreational tobacco can be written off. This includes nicotine patches and nicotine gum, although probably not an extra bottle of wine.

- Being a mortician is a strange profession, and it sometimes attracts odd people. One cadaver specialist proved this when he tried, and failed, to deduct the cost of a tattoo designed to ward off evil spirits from the dead. He said it was necessary for his security; the IRS did not agree.

- Texas wants its citizens to support the "celebration industry." People who enlist the services of a decorating company to put up their Christmas lights and lawn attractions can write off the entire cost on their next tax return. The government doesn't give anything to Texans who want to trim their own tree.

- Hunters are responsible for paying almost $250 million every year in gaming taxes. The taxes go to maintaining and acquiring new public game lands.

Tax Evasionist

The Tax Evasionist is a clever evolution of a classic gin and tonic. It has a kick complimented by ginger and a strong citrus presence. This drink is for taxpayers who don't want to mess around.

Ingredients:
1 ½ Ole Smoky Blackberry Moonshine whiskey
1 ½ Ole Smoky White Lightnin' rum
2 oz. ginger beer
½ oz. lime juice
Fresh mint
Lime slice, optional

Mixing Instructions:
Combine whiskey, rum, and ginger beer in a shaker. Shake well and add ice chips and lime juice. Swirl the mixture slowly before straining out the ice. Pour into a glass; add a mint leaf. Garnish with a slice of lime, if desired.

While the relationship to a gin and tonic is apparent, the Tax
Evasionist is not married to this taste. Various flavored sodas—any
IZZE or Fresca, for instance—will work. As usual, making the right
Tax Evasionist for you takes a little practice and some tweaking to
get right.

"Too much of anything is bad. But too much good whiskey is
barely enough." *–Mark Twain*

"I wish they'd stop increasing the
amount of tax I have to evade."

Luxury Tax

As this book has already shown, people get creative trying to write luxury items off their taxes. The Luxury Tax is just as creative as those excuses, but you won't want to write it off your drink repertoire anytime soon. Make sure to wear only your finest when sipping one of these exquisite creations.

Ingredients:
2 ½ oz. Old Overholt rye whiskey
½ oz. simple syrup
¼ oz. lemon juice
¼ oz. lime juice
3 dashes Peychaud's bitters
Lemon wedge for garnish

Mixing Instructions:
Combine all the ingredients in a blender along with a cup of ice. Blend on high speed until the mixture is completely smooth. Stir with a silver spoon. Pour into a highball glass and garnish with a lemon wedge.

Note: Simple syrup is basically sugar water and is easy to make yourself. Boil water, dissolve an equal amount of white sugar, and let it cool in the fridge for about an hour. Keep it cold or the syrup may start to crystalize.

Rye whiskey is recommended, as you need a strong whiskey to support this drink; Knob Creek and WhistlePig rye are good alternatives. Angostura and Suze bitters can make an interesting substitute for the Peychaud's. Finally, if the lemon/lime/syrup combination isn't to your liking, switching them out for an ounce of root beer can make for a delicious change.

- When the IRS found discrepancies with hotel magnate Leona Helmsley's tax filings, she defended herself by saying, "We don't pay taxes. Only the little people pay taxes." The government put her attitude to the test when they charged Ms. Helmsley with tax fraud. She gave in and paid her debt but never spoke about how much of a "big person" she felt like again.

- Moving from a warm state like California to Minnesota, one of the snowier states in the country, can be difficult. However, the IRS is not going to help make your transition easier. A California family tried to write off the costs of boots, jackets, and even a snow blower before they even reached their destination, unsuccessfully claiming those items as travel expenses.

- Some people consider street performers a nuisance; others, a pleasant feature that lights up downtown. Vermont falls squarely into the former category. Despite the practice being common to down-and-out musicians and other struggling entertainers, Vermont feels the need to take a little more of their earnings away. Some unlucky artists have even faced audits for lack of payment.

"WE DID A GREAT JOB OBTAINING NON-PROFIT TAX STATUS. THAT CALLS FOR BONUSES ALL AROUND!"

- If you drive an electric car to save money on gas, Washington is not the state to live. Every completely green vehicle owner now must pay an extra fee come tax season. The state defends this as necessary for upkeep of the roads in place of the gas tax other drivers contribute. Justifiable? Maybe, but many environmentally friendly motorists aren't pleased.

- The IRS wants as many taxpayers alive as possible. If doctors recommend medication that could substantially extend your life, you may be able to write off the entire cost.

- Mississippi parents successfully deducted the cost of clarinet lessons for their son. Their reason was questionable. A dentist recommended practicing the clarinet to improve the child's overbite. Hopefully they didn't end up having to pay their doctor to correct hearing damage once lessons started.

Charitable Donation

Not unlike literal charity, the Charitable Donation will always show returns, especially around tax season. Who knows? Maybe you can get away with deducting the ingredients for a few of these as a business expense.

Ingredients:

1 ½ oz. Ole Smoky Apple Pie Moonshine whiskey

1 oz. Bacardi Big Apple rum

2 ½ oz. ginger ale

¼ oz. nutmeg

1 apple slice

Mixing Instructions:

Combine moonshine and rum in a shaker with ice. Mix well, remove the ice, add ginger ale, and mix again. Pour the combination into a glass and sprinkle nutmeg on top. Add a small scoop of chipped ice and garnish with a slice of apple.

The Charitable Donation is sweet but deceptively strong. The aggressive apple flavors mask the rum and moonshine past what you might expect. Finishing more than one or two of these could leave you with a headache in the morning. For a toned-down alternative, substitute hard apple cider or even regular cider for the rum.

- A 2016 New Yorker had some very bad luck while gambling in Atlantic City. His fortunes didn't improve when he tried to write off all the money he lost as a charitable contribution to the casino. No doubt he helped fill the house safe with his hard-earned cash, but no one's calling that charity.

- There is a lot to gain in burning down your house. People who donate their home to the local fire department to practice putting fires out can claim the value of the property as a charitable donation. Many a creaky old building has paid dividends for its owner simply by getting torched. For some reason, however, you aren't allowed to set fire to your own business in the middle of the night and call it a charitable donation.

Richard Pryor

The Richard Pryor isn't complicated. It only has a few parts to work with, so cleanup won't take more than a few minutes—not unlike a quality tax shelter for your finances. Remember to talk business with all your local bartenders. That way you can deduct each of your drinking establishments as your place of business.

Ingredients:

1 ½ oz. apple vodka
½ oz. lime juice
½ oz. simple syrup
2 basil leaves
Crumpled dollar bills

Mixing Instructions:

Combine vodka, lime juice, and simple syrup in a mixer. Shake well and pour into a chilled glass. Garnish with two basil leaves. If desired, add ice shavings to keep cool. Float crumpled dollar bills on top to stand in for your past-due reimbursement.

The apple and lime combination is tasty, but there are plenty more blends to try If you prefer. Cîroc, Absolut, and Smirnoff all make a range of high-quality, cheap vodkas with numerous flavors, including apple, orange, pineapple, strawberry, and lemon. Substitute lime juice for orange, apple, or mango juice. If the flavor of juice differs from the vodka variety, you should enjoy the result.

- An ad agency trying to come up with a good campaign for a wine company successful deducted multiple cases of wine from their client's major competitors. They claimed it was "opposition research" and so a necessary business expense. The IRS agreed, and the ad agency stocked their office cost free.

- Legendary comedian Richard Pryor had numerous problems with his taxes. After being charged with evasion, he told a judge, "You know, I just forgot," but Pryor's comedy stylings were not enough to get him out of trouble. The highlight of his issues was spending ten days in jail, enough to jog his memory for the coming tax seasons. Americans collectively paid the IRS close to $5 trillion last year. This total is greater than the amount people spent on food, clothing, and housing combined. While some of that money went back to taxpayers who paid too much, most stayed in the hands of the feds.

The apple and lime cocktail which is tart, but sweet are plenty more. Feel free to experiment, adjust, and add a twist of something different. The recipe is equally tasty with lime, lemon, or orange. Use apple-orange, pineapple-orange, or pear, and lime. Substitute the juice for apple or orange juice. In the flavor of a juice differs from one to another variety, and should alter the result.

Part 3:

Time to Get Tricky: Advanced Cocktails

The previous section covered some relatively straightforward recipes, usually with only one or two alcohols. Part 3 will stretch your skills a little further, use more components, and sometimes require a brewing period.

"You may have fooled us last time, Mr. Chicken, but playing dead won't work this time."

Willie Nelson

Like any IRS bureaucratic nightmare, the Willie Nelson takes awhile. Unlike anything to do with the IRS, this drink is rewarding once you finish.

Ingredients:
1 quart strawberries
1 pint white sugar
1 oz. Citadelle gin
½ oz. Pineau des Charentes aperitif
½ oz. Salers aperitif
1 oz. lemon juice
Basil, lemon, or lime for garnish

Mixing Instructions:
Part 1: Before mixing the drink, you need to prepare strawberry cordial. In a one-quart container, cover strawberries with sugar; let mixture sit overnight at room temperature. Periodically turn the mixture while it sits. After twenty-four hours, strain out the strawberries and leftover sugar, and let the remaining liquid chill until cold.

Part 2: In a tall glass, mix ½ ounce of the strawberry cordial, the alcohols, and the lemon juice. Add a few small ice cubes and stir lightly. Garnish with basil, lemon, or lime as desired.

The Taxman's Delight is extremely customizable; you can really make it your own drink. Virtually any berry works for the cordial; pitted cherries can be particularly delicious. Most gin will work as well, although stay away from anything too dry like Bombay Sapphire or Tanqueray.

- A couple in Maine successfully deducted all expenses related to a private plane they owned. They had an upstate property for rent but did not want to consistently drive seven hours to check on it. The two took the obvious course of action and purchased a fully furnished jet to cut down on the commute. Next tax season, the IRS agreed to foot the bill for all fuel and upkeep.

- It is not uncommon for states to set a fall weekend where back-to-school items are tax free. Virginia took this idea a few steps further and included some purchases of questionable educational value. The potential exemptions included fur coats, aprons, corsets, garters, and even lingerie. Some Virginia legislators may have had unconventional school experiences.

- Nineteen-ninety saw one of the most infamous celebrity tax debts on record when country singer Willie Nelson suddenly found he owed the IRS a whopping $17 million in back taxes. He had to sell most of his possessions to cover the debt, including several treasured antique guitars. Afterward, through contributions and special auctions, his fans helped him buy back most of what he had sold.

Tax Collector

If you want to match a tax collector's spirit in spirits, the Tax Collector is appropriate. This witch's brew has five different alcohols and makes enough to stun a team of oxen. So, when the tax agent comes a knockin', serve him a few of these and you will be able to make a hasty escape out the back door (or even the front door). He won't be in any condition to follow you.

Ingredients:

2 oz. gin	8 oz. orange juice
1 oz. dark rum	10 oz. pineapple juice
2 oz. 151 proof rum	3 oz. lemon juice
2 oz. light rum	4 pineapple chunks
2 oz. vodka	8 maraschino cherries
2 oz. grenadine	

Mixing Instructions:

Combine gin, all three rums, vodka, grenadine, and all three juices in a large blender with 3 cups of ice. Blend on high until mixture is uniform. You can divvy up the resulting 32-ounce concoction in however many servings you want, but 8 ounces should be plenty. Garnish each drink with pineapple and cherries as desired.

Because of its numerous liquors, the Tax Collector does not require particularly nuanced alcohol selections. Any gin, vodka, or varieties of dark, light, and 151 rums will do. Of course, you can experiment with changes in types of juice or alcohol/mix proportion. Instead of straight vodka, soak twenty gummy bears in vodka overnight and add them to the mixture as the final step. This makes for a great group drink, maybe for a post–tax season celebration.

Taxman Runs the Debtor Down

The Debtor Down is a phenomenal beverage that can be a lot of fun to make and even more enjoyable to drink. As with the Taxman's Delight, this beverage will take a time commitment to do properly, but it's worth the effort. This is also our first venture into flame-infused drinks. Like a guilty party under audit, tread carefully when concocting this one.

Ingredients:

4 overripe bananas

2 tbsp. white sugar

1 cinnamon stick

1 liter bourbon

6 blueberries

2 tbsp. brown sugar

Splash of 151 proof rum

Dash cinnamon

Mixing Instructions:

Part 1: Peel the bananas, cut them into ½-inch sections, and top with sugar. Set the mixture in a large jar with the cinnamon stick, then pour on the bourbon. Seal the jar and let it chill in the fridge for at least two days, a week if possible. After the bourbon is fully infused, strain well to remove the remaining banana and cinnamon. Let it sit for another hour before straining again.

Part 2: In a fire-safe cup, preferably a stainless-steel julep cup, combine the blueberries and brown sugar, then add a dash of rum on top. Fire the rum and immediately sprinkle the ground cinnamon on top; be aware of sparks. Use a muddler or other fire-safe mashing tool to crush the mixture well and extinguish the flame. Add three ounces of the banana-infused bourbon and a handful of crushed ice. Stir well and top with some fire-extinguisher spray for show.

Lighting fire to something you are about to drink may be intimidating, but it's quite easy if you pay attention. The key to a good Taxman Runs the Debtor Down is properly infusing the bourbon; it takes time to bring out the whole pallet. Of course, banana-flavored bourbon is available at most well-stocked liquor stores, but it won't be nearly as potent.

- Every year, Wisconsin gets to break federal law. Taxing internet access is illegal nationwide, but Wisconsin has government permission to continue this tax, as it was passed before Congress legislated against it.

- Wyoming is a great place for Americans with a sweet tooth. Any candy purchased in the state is fully exempt from income tax. The same goes for gift baskets that are at least half full of candy.

- In an unconventional attempt to stay current, the Rhode Island government has added smiley-face emoticons to its income tax forms. There may be the odd Rhode Islander cheered up by a sad emoji next to the "amount due" space, but most filers are purportedly mystified by this sudden update.

- A surprising and deeply satisfying twist in tax history occurred when former IRS Commissioner Joseph D. Nunan was convicted of evasion following his tenure with the federal government. He found himself in hot water after failing to report $1,800 he won betting that Harry Truman would become president. It's rare that an employee gets revenge on their former boss in such a humiliating manner, but there were probably some smiling faces at the IRS offices when Mr. Nunan found himself in hot water.

- An inventive North Carolinian who ran a business out of his house suddenly found he could write off all his dog-related expenses by claiming the pet pup was there for "office security" and therefore, a business expense. Now you can add "tax benefits" to the list of reasons a dog really is mankind's best friend.

Contrary to popular belief, the road to Hell is paved with a comprehensive, lifetime tax return.

Wily Withholder

Not unlike this drink, withholding your income tax is a great way to set your mind at ease. No one wants the specter of a federal investigation in their life. The Wily Withholder will whisk you away from the stress of tax season.

Ingredients:

½ oz. 151 proof rum
1 oz. pineapple juice
1 oz. orange juice
½ oz. apricot brandy
1 tsp. white sugar
2 oz. light rum
1 oz. dark rum
1 oz. lime juice
1 lime slice for garnish

Mixing Instructions:

Combine all ingredients except the 151 proof rum in a blender. Add a cup of ice and blend on high until the mixture is uniform. Pour your drink into a glass and float the remaining rum on top. Garnish with a lime slice. This drink is best served in a glass with Wile E. Coyote stickers on it.

The Wily Withholder is the first drink featured here that really makes use of varying drink densities. If done properly, the denser mixture should stay on the bottom of the glass while the rum sits on top without combining. This style looks impressive and provides an excellent two-part taste.

- Washington, DC, has made some seriously odd choices when it comes to what to tax. The legislature tacked on a 6% tax that applies only to gyms and sugary drinks. If you want to save money in DC, just stay in average shape.

- In 2017, one Minnesota resident attempted to deduct his kid's high school graduation party. He claimed it was a "future business expense." Supposedly, the relationships the child made at her party would help her start a business after college. The IRS did not oblige him.

- In "adult" industries, the IRS has a clear policy accepting breast implants as a business expense, but there is a catch. The government considers implants an asset of depreciating value, and every year actresses and dancers everywhere are required to deduct a little less for their investment.

Uncle Sam's Pumpkin Punch Write-Off

This masterpiece might be the greatest challenge this book has to offer. Like the Tax Collector, finishing this drink is not a solo operation; it will require at least eight people to drink in one evening. You can declare them all as dependents by the end of the night; your guests may end up sleeping on the couch. Uncle Sam's Pumpkin Punch Write-Off is perfect for a fall party.

Ingredients:

1 small pumpkin	18 oz. Elijah Craig bourbon
2 tsp. cardamom	8 oz. ginger liqueur
1 tsp. nutmeg	6 tbsp. pumpkin puree
3 cinnamon sticks	12 oz. apple juice
3 crushed cloves	12 oz. pineapple juice
Splash of orange juice	12 oz. lemon juice
2 cups white sugar	

Mixing Instructions:

Part 1: Cut the top third of the pumpkin off. Remove all seeds and pumpkin pulp. Ensure the inside is **completely** empty.

Part 2: Toast cardamom in a pan on medium heat. Stir in spices, orange juice, sugar, and 2 cups of water. Let the mixture cool, then strain it into a mason jar.

Part 3: Combine bourbon, liqueur, puree, 4 ounces of the syrup made in part 2, and all three juices in the pumpkin. Add ice and stir well. It is essential the pumpkin is cleaned fully; no one wants seeds floating in their glass.

- Some states clearly favor Thanksgiving over Halloween. Iowa, New Jersey, and Pennsylvania allow for people to write off the cost of pumpkins, but only if eaten. People who buy pumpkins to carve are out of luck. So, homemade pumpkin pie is big in Iowa. Jack-o-lanterns? Maybe not as much.

- In 2017, one well-armed Minnesotan inexplicably decided to donate a set of chainsaws to a children's hospital. What he had in mind when making this contribution is anyone's guess, but despite the hospital accepting his donation, the IRS did not allow him to write off the cost.

Boston Tea Party

Americans have been protesting unfair taxes for hundreds of years. Unfortunately, you can't show your displeasure by dumping barrels of tea into a harbor anymore. Take the edge off with this drink inspired by one of the most famous tax protests in history.

Ingredients:

3 oz. green tea leaves
20 oz. honey
1 ½ oz. bourbon
½ oz. white wine (see suggestions)
¾ oz. lemon juice
1 egg white
1 dash Angostura bitters
*Optional: water from Boston Harbor

Mixing Instructions:

Part 1: Steep tea in 10 oz. water—preferably imported from Boston—for 15 minutes. Strain out the tea leaves and stir in honey while the tea is still warm. Let the mixture cool before use.

Part 2: Combine bourbon, wine, ¾ oz. of the tea syrup, lemon juice, and egg white in a shaker. Shake, and pour into a glass. Stir in the bitters slowly without disrupting the foam that should have gathered.

Recommended white wine is Chambers Muscadelle, but any potent white with strong citrus or honey flavors will do the job. Bulleit straight will do for the bourbon, although any type is fine, as most of the flavor is shaped by the tea syrup and wine.

- Anyone who plans on renting out a home should be aware: if guests pay for fifteen days or less, your income is tax free. However, if your visitors fork over even one dollar on day 16, all income is subject to regular federal rental taxes.

- Every year, Americans claim deductions for loans to family members and the IRS denies their claims. However, if you get official confirmation of the loan in writing, the IRS allows up to $3,000 a year in deductions until you are paid back.

Part 4:

Heating Up with Hot Toddies

So far, this book has dealt with drinks served cool, either with ice or in a chilled glass. However, heat can have a big role in the perfect cocktail as well. Part 4 is all about toddies and even drinks that play with fire. Just be careful that fire doesn't spread its way onto tax forms.

EZ Form

Sometimes a little chocolate-infused buzz is what you need to keep going throughout a stressful tax process. In that case, this easy-to-mix cocktail is the perfect choice.

Ingredients:

1 oz. Irish cream Kahlúa
1 oz. crème de cacao
4 oz. hot chocolate
1 dash nutmeg

Mixing Instructions:

Combine Kahlúa, crème de cacao, and hot chocolate in a mug. Sprinkle nutmeg on top and swirl the mixture slightly. Drink it hot.

The EZ Form is a straightforward drink, but several add-ons can make it a bit more elaborate, if you are inclined. Many prefer something a little stronger; in that case, add an ounce of whiskey and an ounce of hot chocolate. Others with a sweet tooth will top off their creation with a spray of whipped cream. Finally, if you want a nice coffee flavor to augment the EZ Form, add a shot of espresso. Mash up a few Whoppers and mix them in for extra sweetness.

Red Flag

Sometimes taxpayer behavior will set off alerts at the Internal Revenue Service. If you're caught in the middle of that, it might be time to warm up and get ready to leave with a different type of Red Flag.

Ingredients:

1 ¼ oz. 2% milk
¾ oz. cherry liqueur
¾ oz. cream
¾ oz. white rum
1 pair running shoes

Mixing Instructions:

Heat milk in a saucepan until warm. Combine the milk, liqueur, cream, and rum in a heat-resistant mug. Wait for the cocktail to slightly cool before drinking, then put on the sneakers and start running! For extra zip, grab some jet fuel next time you're at an airport. Add 2 ounces of jet fuel to the Red Flag and you'll really be ready to move.

The Red Flag is not complex, but be careful not to heat the milk too long. You don't want it steaming before you combine it with the other ingredients. Don't stray too far from white rum if you need to substitute for another variety. Overproof rum, 151-proof or higher, is almost as bad as vodka for a Red Flag, and vodka is a *very* bad choice here. Any type of well-made running shoe should do.

- The very wealthy pay a high percentage in taxes these days. The peak bracket is about 40%, but it has been much higher at times. Following the early days of World War II, some of America's richest citizens were giving up as much as 94% of their income to support the war effort. President Roosevelt advocated for a 100% marginal income tax rate on the rich, which he would have been subject to, but was shot down in Congress.

- It goes without saying that astronauts often must maintain an incredible level of focus in their work. They are operating the most advanced machines ever built for extremely unstable conditions. However, the IRS can distract even the most hardened space traveler. Jack Swigert, a pilot for the Apollo 13 mission, forgot to file his taxes and earnestly asked mission control about his liability while in the space capsule. The IRS ultimately gave him a pass.

- The IRS will reward you for ratting out wealthy evaders. If you point the government toward a significant source of revenue they've been missing, they might deduct as much as 30% of what they get from your target off your taxes. That's a healthy deduction, but do you really want to be on the side of the IRS?

Appeal Adjustment

If you get lucky and the IRS forks over a little extra dough after an appeal, a celebration is in order. This is the perfect drink to commemorate the occasion.

Ingredients:

2 oz. dark rum

¾ oz. Calvados brandy

1 tbsp. maple syrup

5 oz. hot milk

1 cinnamon stick

1 dash nutmeg

1 dash cinnamon

Mixing Instructions:

Combine rum, brandy, and maple syrup in a mug or heat-resistant glass. Fill with warm milk and stir well with the cinnamon stick. Sprinkle with a dash of nutmeg and cinnamon. Continue stirring with the cinnamon stick while you drink.

This toasty concoction is a great way to fight cold weather and get a little buzz at the same time. For a little more kick, lower the milk content, but don't go below 3 ½ oz. If your successful appeal has come through, use some of the money from your return with this drink. Sniff some dollar bills, preferably $50s, although $20s will do, before every drink. The smell of money always pairs well with brandy.

- In 1987, the IRS was sick of catching people who claimed nonexistent children as dependents. They added a stipulation that the filer have their dependent's social security number on the tax form they were submitting. The next year, almost 10% of American children "disappeared" from tax records, never to return.

- Madison Square Garden in New York is an international icon, but it does not bring in nearly as many tax dollars for the city as it could. A tax break set up in 1982 as a temporary measure to help the venue when it was struggling financially was poorly written, and due to clever legal maneuvers, MSG hasn't paid property taxes since. In 2016 alone, New York lost approximately $48 million due to this absent revenue.

It's Time to Sell the Jet Ski

If the feds have you for a lot of back taxes, you might need to start selling some luxury items to pay them back. That's never fun, but it will be a lot easier if you down an It's Time to Sell the Jet Ski first. This recipe makes enough for ten, but how you distribute them should be in proportion to how much each person will have to sell to cover their debts.

Ingredients:
16 oz. pecans
1 liter scotch
¾ red wine
2 cups apple cider
¾ cup honey syrup
2 cinnamon sticks

Mixing Instructions:
Part 1: Place pecans on a baking sheet and lightly sprinkle them with salt and pepper. Roast at 200 degrees for 25 minutes. After letting them cool, pour pecans into airtight container with the scotch. Let mixture sit for a week and then strain out the leftover solids.

Part 2: Combine 1 ½ ounces of the pecan-infused scotch with the rest of the ingredients in a pan and bring them to a boil. Reduce the heat to low for one hour. Strain out the cinnamon sticks. Drink in mugs while the mixture is warm. If you are hurting for a few extra dollars, you could probably sell this under the table for good money; just make sure not to get caught bootlegging.

I.R.S. Training Center

Roy Delgado

"... and then you smile and say... all together now... 'that's not deductible'."

"I'm sorry, but to lower your taxes you're going to have to make more money."

- As noted before, FDR was crazy for raising income taxes. In 1939, he raised the marginal income tax rate for the highest bracket to 79%. The rate only applied to people making $5 million a year or more. In the entire country, only one man qualified for the new tax bracket: John D. Rockefeller.

- Most states impose a "jock tax" for professional athletes who are staying in cities briefly to play games. That means whenever the Yankees head south to face off against the Red Sox, Aaron Judge is forking over a little extra cash for a hot dog. Maybe that's why he needs millions of dollars a year.

- For a reason which is now forgotten, the federal government places a higher tax on figurines of humans. Of course, this affects comic book companies more than any other business, and Marvel Comics' lawyers went to court to fight this tax. Their argument? Many of the company's characters were technically mutants and therefore only resembled humans. They won the case and have saved millions as a result.

Al Capone

This warm confection is a potent relative of prohibition-era cocktails, drinks made in back rooms outside the law. Just don't get caught dodging your taxes while drinking it.

Ingredients:
3 oz. rye whiskey
4 oz. black coffee

Mixing Instructions:
Combine ingredients in a tall glass; serve warm. An Al Capone is best drunk in a suit, with a tilted fedora, expensive cigar, and even a Thompson .45 submachine gun, if you really want to get into the spirit of it.

Whether it's early in the morning or late at night, if you're not feeling alert, the Al Capone will perk you right up. The strength of the rye whiskey might be a bit much for weary drinkers, so adding an ounce of coffee is a reasonable idea. Don't decrease the whiskey, as you'll need that to stay sharp and ready for the feds.

"Whiskey is liquid sunshine." *–George Bernard Shaw*

- The IRS recently hit a milestone when it comes to paperwork. As of 2015, there are over two thousand different forms available to taxpayers on the IRS website. As if the bureaucracy isn't big enough, that number is still growing today.

- The popular TV program *Breaking Bad* is about a chemistry teacher turned drug dealer in New Mexico. California was the original setting for the show, but New Mexico has much more lenient tax laws. *Breaking Bad's* creators insisted on shooting on-site, so the show ended up set in Albuquerque, thanks to the federal tax code.

- The notorious gangster Al Capone made his fortune as a rum-runner during the prohibition era of the 1920s. Eventually, an alert agent of the US treasury realized Capone hadn't been paying taxes for years and he was arrested for evasion. Capone's time keeping Americans boozy was up. Lucky for drinkers everywhere, prohibition was soon over, and nobody went long without their hooch.

Crafty Concealment

This mixture, like a lot of tax return "meddling," is hot. Somewhere in the legal grey area between breaking the law and having an "intimate understanding of the tax code," you might find a few lucky breaks for your yearly return. The Crafty Concealment is a drink for such times.

Ingredients:

4 oz. porter or stout beer

1 ½ oz. whiskey

½ oz. root beer syrup

Whipped cream

Mixing Instructions:

Warm the beer on the stove until hot. Pour into a glass and stir in the whiskey and root beer syrup. Top with a spray of whipped cream.

Mostly the whiskey is just there for a kick, but Jameson or something else Irish is ideal if you want to be choosey. Many people are shy about trying warm beer, but with the right ingredients, it can make for a great mix. Make sure to use dark beer, nothing too light or fruity. Suds that are too clear don't match the spirit or *spirit* of the Crafty Concealment.

"Beauty is in the eye of the beer holder." —*Kinky Friedman*

- The length of the full federal tax code has long been the subject of ridicule, given its rapid growth and rise in complexity. Currently, there are 3.7 million words of tax rules. That is more than five times the length of the Bible.

- Some companies are doing a great job at avoiding IRS interference in their finances. In 2010, the company General Electric took in $4 billion in profits in the United States and didn't pay a nickel in taxes. If they could teach some other Americans how to do that, everyone might be a lot happier.

- As many New Yorkers know, it is tough to be a smoker in the Big Apple. Rhode Island and New Jersey have the second and third highest taxes on cigarettes in the US at $3.47 and $2.70. In New York City, the combined city and state tax brings the total tax to an impressive $4.25.

Part 5:

Novelties

Now it's time to get into the more eccentric areas of mixology. A five-tier layered rainbow shot makes for an inspired visual presentation, or at least something nice to distract yourself with after the IRS has gutted last year's earnings. The same is true for iridescent glow-in-the-dark cocktails and anything where your drink is on fire for extended periods of time.

" That's the way Dad does it on his income tax. "

Chocolate Bacon Bourbon Bankruptcy Deluxe

If you can find anything like this in a bar, it might not be a good establishment to drink at. Don't go looking for these in normal society; avoid publicly served bacon bourbon like you would bankruptcy.

Ingredients:

5 strips cooked bacon

1 liter bourbon

1 oz. milk

1 tsp. powdered chocolate milk mix

1 tsp. cinnamon

Mixing Instructions:

Part 1: Cook the bacon, and after letting it cool, seal four strips in a tight container with the bourbon. Let the mixture stand for a week. Strain out the solids.

Part 2: Combine milk and chocolate milk mix in a highball glass. After stirring well, add 1 ½ ounces of the bacon-infused bourbon. Mix in cinnamon and stir it with the remaining slice of bacon.

Keep snacking on bacon while you drink this. If you get high-quality meat, preferably cut in thick strips and with a maple glaze, the taste profile is shockingly good. Don't cook the bacon too much. It will just break apart in the bourbon if it's overly crispy. The strips should be a little floppy still, although not greasy.

"My horoscope says I'll be noticed by people who count."

Nicolas Cage

This blazing shot is engulfed in flames as you drink it, so you're going to need a straw and a helper. Like an out-of-control performance from Nicolas Cage, this drink will draw attention. Fortunately, the attention will be from nearby bargoers, not the IRS.

Ingredients:

1 oz. Kahlúa

1 oz. sambuca

1 oz. blue curaçao

1 oz. Baileys Irish Cream

Mixing Instructions:

Assemble a cocktail glass and two shot glasses side by side. Fill the cocktail glass with Kahlúa then sambuca, and drop in a straw. Fill the shot glasses with blue curaçao and Baileys (separately, not half/half). With a lighter, set the cocktail glass mixture on fire and have the subject start drinking through the straw. When almost finished, pour in the shots and have them drink until completed.

The Nicolas Cage is a lot of fun, especially with a group. Whoever is pouring needs to pay attention, and the drinker can't take their time. However, in the end, it's not that hard to pull off and is a great way to blow off some steam.

- Yearly tax filings don't only bring in money for a government, they provide a huge revenue stream for the tax service industry. Collectively, Americans spent over $26 billion on tax software and accountants in 2016.

- The comedian Sinbad, known for his audacious antics both on and off stage, was in deep with the IRS for many years, owing the IRS as much as $2.5 million in 2013. Unlike many other tax dodgers, Sinbad later said he didn't regret any of the behavior that led to his losses. He claimed, "I didn't live large; I invested in me. I invested in many other people. I wouldn't change it. I wouldn't go back."

- Actor Nicolas Cage's net worth is estimated at an impressive $25 million. This is made even more remarkable by the fact that he owes the IRS $7.2 million, and that's for 2007 alone. He is rumored to owe much more. This eye-popping level of debt might explain Cage's notorious enthusiasm in every movie he's in.

Barbequed Tax Burden

When the mountain of taxes you're forced to fork over seems crushing and you feel like the IRS is virtually roasting you over an open flame with all their stipulations and hidden fees, it's time for a drink. The Barbequed Tax Burden is a strange one, no doubt, but tax time calls for extreme measures.

Ingredients:
5 oz. barbeque sauce
5 oz. water
1 ½ oz. bourbon
1 oz. honey whiskey liqueur
¼ orange, juiced
12 oz. beer

Mixing Instructions:
Part 1: Combine barbeque sauce in a mixing bowl with the water. Stir well and let sit in the refrigerator until cool.

Part 2: Fill a mixer with ice, liquors, and one ounce of the barbeque water. Squeeze the orange juice in as well. Shake well, strain out the ice, and pour it into a cocktail glass. Add a quarter of the beer to the mixer, and mix intensely until the beer is very foamy. Scoop off a spoonful of foam and spread it on top of the cocktail.

For something a little simpler, forget about the beer, BBQ water, liqueur, orange, ice, mixer, and glass, and just take pulls of straight bourbon from the bottle. After a few healthy swigs, you won't notice a difference.

"I cook with wine. Sometimes I even add it to the food."

–W.C. Fields

- While some people know the stories of Al Capone and Willie Nelson already, Walter Anderson may be the greatest tax evader in history, and he's not gotten much credit from the public. A telecommunications entrepreneur, Anderson hid a half-billion-dollar income from the government for years in offshore accounts. When he was ultimately caught, Anderson ended up paying a combined $400 million in taxes and fines.

- Texas made an odd choice when it comes to exotic dancers. Every strip club in the Lone Star State should be thrift when it comes to poles; the state government adds a $5 tax every year to each stripper poll an establishment has up.

- If income taxes seem extreme to you, it might be because they started as a war measure. During the Civil War, the Union army needed more money to pay for supplies. To fund the war effort and encourage enlistment, the federal government started taking a percentage of every civilian wage.

Floating Baldwin

Sometimes taxes just don't swing your way and there's nothing that can be done. When the inevitable is about to strike, a frustrated citizen can chill out with a Floating Baldwin.

Ingredients:
1 large scoop vanilla ice cream
12 oz. beer (non-light)
Chocolate sauce
1 dash cinnamon

Mixing Instructions:
Make sure that all your light beer is in the trash before mixing, as it could affect the taste if too close. Drop the ice cream into a large glass. Pour a 12-oz beer over it and mix until there is a healthy froth of foam. Drizzle chocolate sauce over the ice cream. Sprinkle the dash of cinnamon on top.

The Floating Baldwin is all about the beer you choose. Darker is better, although an ale or something fruity will work well too. Feel free to add a fruit as a garnish in that case, but don't go overboard; this isn't punch. If you use a light beer, this will taste bad.

- The tax filing assistance industry is prosperous enough to hold significant sway in politics. In 2016, H&R Block and Intuit—makers of TurboTax—spent upward of $5 million lobbying the US congress to keep tax forms and filing as complex as possible, and even to increase the intricacies of tax forms. Lengthy tax paperwork leaves many people confused and frustrated and thus more willing to pay for help. Next time you're upset about completing endless tax forms, remember to thank TurboTax for their continued complexity.

- Stephen Baldwin, of *The Usual Suspects* and *Born on the Fourth of July* fame, has had numerous problems with the IRS regarding inconsistent returns. In 2010, he was charged with not paying New York state taxes for three years to the tune of $400,000. He recently managed to pay what he owed, but that wasn't lesson enough. In 2015, the feds caught him for another ninety grand. He might have been taking his role as a well-known criminal in *Usual Suspects* too far.

- In 2016, the average tax return was roughly $2,750, with 74% of taxpayers getting at least a little cash back. If you end up getting roughed-up by the IRS this year, at least you're not alone.

The Stinky Abatement

Everyone appreciates an abatement, but some of them stink a little. Maybe you're feeling a little guilty about an unfair refund or slightly worried that the IRS will catch on to some tax dodge you've pulled off. The Stinky Abatement is all that turned into one foul drink.

Ingredients:

16 oz. linguine noodles

2 oz. brie cheese

2 oz. cheddar cheese

4 oz. 151 proof rum

3 oz. lime juice

½ oz. tomato sauce

Mixing Instructions:

Fully cook the noodles and then mix them and the cheeses in a blender on high until liquified. Pour into a mixer and add the rum and lime juice. Let the mixture sit unrefrigerated for four hours. Before drinking, mix again with uncooked linguini and float tomato sauce on top.

If brie is unavailable, any other cheese will do; just make sure it's soft enough for your blender to handle. Make sure to blend the noodles well, as you don't want any lumps. For maximum taste, add pickled eggs, old socks, or dirty shoelaces to the blended mixture. You won't forget this drink anytime soon.

- A Florida man was getting numerous complaints from coworkers that his feet smelled to the point of making their jobs more difficult. He bought powder to deal with his unfortunate aroma, but the IRS wasn't accommodating when he tried to write off the cost of the powder as a business expense.

- Darryl Strawberry is a baseball legend. Through the '80s and '90s, he was swatting countless baseballs out of ballparks across the country. Unfortunately, he was also neglecting his taxes. The IRS found that Strawberry owed almost a million dollars in back taxes he accrued during that time.

- Kentucky is the host state for the landmark yearly horse race, the Kentucky Derby. As a result, the Bluegrass State has a bustling horse-trading and breeding industry. The state is capitalizing on this by imposing a 6% sales tax on stud fees. They then redistribute this money through several incentive programs to keep the industry local.

- In Wisconsin, the government favors modern baby-clothing methods. Parents who prefer to use cloth diapers on their babies must pay taxes for this essential item. Disposable diapers, however, are free of sales tax and so even less expensive.

- The IRS has one of the most complex tax bureau-cracies in existence, and it doesn't come cheap to process. They spend roughly $2.45 of your money for every $100 they collect.

- If you are not a fan of government outlay, you may be happy to hear tax evaders have had a major impact on the national income. Since 2006, studies indicate the US government has lost a total of $3.1 billion. That's a lot of spending.

Four-Tiered Financer

This shot features an impressive visual display with five discrete colors layered on top of one another in one glass. Successfully making a Four-Tiered Financer takes patience, five kinds of liqueur, and a steady hand.

Ingredients:

½ oz. Kahlúa

½ oz. Midori

½ oz. Irish cream

½ oz. Jägermeister

½ oz. 50 dollars in blended cash

Mixing Instructions:

In a double shot glass, *slowly* pour each of the liquors—first the Kahlúa, then Midori, then Irish cream, then Jäger. Very carefully, sprinkle the blended cash on top. Your goal is to keep each layer from mixing. If you go too fast, the layers will start to seep together and you'll end up with a double shot of brownish sludge. Creating this drink is all about taking your time.

Legend has it that the blended cash acts as a sacrifice to the tax gods. By drinking some of your own money along with this visually stunning shot, you can bring good luck every tax season. A loss of $50 at least is necessary; anything less would be an insult.

- Oregon recently legalized the sale of marijuana for recreational use, and they are ready to capitalize on this rare tax opportunity. The government added a whopping 25% sales tax on all marijuana sold in drug dispensaries. In part due to this tax, illegal drug dealers are still very much a part of Oregonian society.

- Whatever you think of Al Sharpton's politics, there is no doubt he has had some run-ins with the law. In 1989 the IRS charged him with tax evasion. While he was ultimately acquitted, suspicions still lingered, and he was charged again in 2009 to the tune of $538,000 in back taxes. Sharpton paid up and hasn't stepped out of line since.

- Vermont is, for some people, the "maple syrup state." This delicious topping is one of the products it's best known for. Maybe the good's success is the reason for an extra 6% sales tax Vermont imposes on each bottle sold.

Sickly Sweet Severance Pay

A severance package can be crucial to keeping a newly fired person afloat. However, the good people at the IRS, in their infinite wisdom, are fine with taxing such an important and short-lived revenue stream. If you're not careful, something that seems like a sweet deal can sour fast come tax time. The Sickly Sweet Severance Pay is the alcoholic version of such a situation.

Ingredients:

5 rolls Smarties

2 Hershey chocolate bars, 1.55 oz.

6 oz. rum

6 oz. pineapple juice

Handful of gummy bears

2 Starbursts

Mixing Instructions:

Part 1: Grind Smarties into powder with a heavy stack of tax forms. Melt Hershey bars in the microwave or a double boiler until completely liquid.

Part 2: Combine rum, pineapple juice, crushed Smarties, and melted Hershey bars in a blender and mix until uniform. Pour into a glass and drop in gummy bears. Garnish with Starbursts and drink from a candy straw. If it's not sweet enough to make you ill, just dump a cup of pure sugar into the concoction; that should do the job.

- The Arkansas government is a little rougher on people who get tattoos and piercings than other states. They apply a 6% sales tax to every tattoo and body piercing; the same tax applies to getting that body art removed.

- Judy Garland, beloved star of *Wizard of Oz* fame, owed the IRS $4 million at one point. That's a ton of money these days, but it was far more substantial in 1964. She lost most of the fortune she earned from playing Dorothy, although ultimately made it back with other films.

- Georgia is not friendly toward cigar owners or manufacturers. They apply a whopping 23% sales tax to all stogies sold in the state. If you've got the habit, you'd better be ready to pay.

Transit Tax Refund

Some states are lenient on taxing modes of transportation. Often, they are a consistent business expense for people who need to get to work every day. This has made for many a nice surprise when it comes to tax return season. The Transit Tax Refund is nothing if not surprising.

Ingredients:
4 oz. tequila
8 oz. chopped honeydew melon
4 oz. strawberries
1 cup ice
4 oz. rum
Parking tickets
Green food coloring

Mixing Instructions:
Part 1: Combine tequila, melon, strawberries, and ice in a blender and mix until smooth. Pour into a large glass.

Part 2: Combine rum, tickets, and food coloring in a blender and mix until smooth if possible. Stir with the stick used to check your car's oil. Pour an ounce of the mixture in with the drink created in part 1.

Unless you have a ton of parking tickets, this drink will look delicious. It won't taste great, so let somebody else drink it. Give it to a friend who is looking for a buzz. Make sure to take a video of them trying it for the first time.

- Kansas favors the unorthodox when it comes to commuting in the clouds. Their tax code includes the stipulation that untethered hot air balloon rides are exempt from state taxes, as they can be considered a form of regular transportation. Tethered hot air balloon rides are supposedly just for entertainment and are therefore subject to sales tax.

- Montana is serious about starting the clean energy movement in the United States. If one of their residents installs a source of renewable energy, that person will receive a 35% tax rebate on all costs related to the appliance.

- Italian actress Sophia Lauren was known for her charm, but for eighteen days she ended up somewhere that clashed with her alluring persona: an Italian prison. She served time for nonpayment of taxes in 1982. For decades, Lauren upheld she was innocent of any wrongdoing, and 2013 saw her justification. A court found that her incarceration was a mistake.

Flaming Tax Forms

Ever hate your taxes so much you just want to burn them? Totally understandable. Do so while having a drink. This drink will require advanced equipment to create.

Ingredients:

1 oz. black sambuca

3 coffee beans

3 oz. 151 proof rum

Mixing Instructions:

Combine sambuca and coffee beans in a shot glass. Light the sambuca on fire with a thermal lance. Let it burn for about ten seconds. Cover the top of the glass with your hand to extinguish the flame. Wait a few seconds, then uncover the top and quickly inhale the air, which will be filled with alcoholic vapor. Drink the remaining liquid in the shot glass. Drink the double shot of rum.

The mixture of sambuca, coffee, and overproof rum flavors will pair well with the gas released by the thermal lance. An average thermal lance heats up to about 4,000 degrees, so be careful of the shot glass cracking. You may want an oven mitt on when you cover the top of the glass.

- A Minnesota man's claim quickly became legendary in the IRS when he reported hiring an arsonist to burn down his business for insurance money. This bold bloke tried to claim the arsonist's fees were a business expense, despite his business now consisting mostly of ashes and cash registers full of money that happened to escape the fire. To no sane observer's surprise, the federal government did not grant him the write-off.

- South Dakota promotes volunteer service in their tax code. Anyone working in a volunteer fire department or ambulance department is not required to pay sales taxes on items relating to their position.

- Accountants, not surprisingly, often count on tax season for their employment. Every year, Americans hire a total of over one million accountants to help manage their taxes.

- H. Ty Warner made a fortune selling millions of his Beanie Babies to a public suddenly crazy over stuffed bear toys. When the craze died down, Warner didn't want to give up any of his wealth and hid it in offshore accounts. Unfortunately, the IRS found out, and he ended up owing $25 million.

- Some relationships can be expensive, and occasionally the IRS is willing to help shoulder that burden. In 2015, a New Jersey man gave his girlfriend $9,000 to furnish an apartment he bought her. The government let him write off $2,500, as his significant other was planning to occasionally rent the property.

- Albert Einstein, the genius behind theories of relativity and many other breakthroughs in physics and chemistry, had a notoriously difficult time dealing with American taxes. He often told friends, "The most difficult thing in the world is understanding the income tax."

"The penny saved is fine. It's this penny earned
we'd like to talk to you about."

Inebriate's Reviled Swill

The Inebriate's Reviled Swill is an untamed combination that defies description. Its potency is limitless, its proof unheard of. It is the IRS, it is illegal in most states, and it will take you out.

> ### *Ingredients:*
> *1 oz. Jack Daniel's green label whiskey*
> *1 oz. Jeppson's Malört*
> *3 oz. Everclear 190 proof grain alcohol*
> *1 splash fresh pomegranate juice*
>
> ### *Mixing Instructions:*
> Combine all ingredients in a highball glass. Chill in a fridge before drinking. Consume it all at once, or not at all.

This drink isn't only strong enough to strip rust off sheet metal or clean a tractor combine, it is difficult to make. To be a true IRS, there is no compromising on ingredients. Jack Daniel's green label is excellent but is no longer sold in most liquor stores and only readily available online. The same is true of Malört, which is exclusive to the Midwest. Unfortunately, many states tightly regulate liquor shipping, so both can be difficult to come by if you live on a coast. You can substitute gasoline for Malört and no one will know the difference.

190 proof Everclear is quite simply illegal in many states. However, if you are determined to make and consume this drink, Illinois has all three liquors available and within the bounds of the law. It will be a genuine testament to your drinking prowess to make and finish the IRS.

"Abandon all hope." –*Creators of the IRS*

- IRS agents sometimes have a dark sense of humor when it comes to the power inherent to their job. Under the cover of anonymity, one employee said, "There is no important piece of information concerning you I am forbidden to seek."

- The state government of Pennsylvania uses its citizens' proclivities to booze it up as an advantage. Legislators have imposed an 18% tax on every bottle of alcohol sold in the state. The money collected as a result will go toward preparing for potential natural disasters.

Note: For those who haven't tried Malört, it legitimately smells like gasoline. No one has verified what gasoline tastes like, but it is probably similar, except less damaging to your health.

Conclusion

This country has come a long way since its founding, both in terms of taxation and drinking. Our government used to survive on a few simple tax laws, and now we have an endless maze of rules and fees to navigate. Our people used to survive on whiskey, for the most part, and now there are thousands of drinks and numerous liqueurs. Each city has a variety of microbrews and local spirits loved by the populous. Do we need that many taxes or alcohols? Maybe not, but at least the latter can take your mind off the former.

In a way, this book is about American exceptionalism. Here, taxes are more demanding and drinking is more creative than in any other nation in history. The government takes, but bartenders give. The taxmen demand their due every year, and every year, mixologists create more wonders to imbibe. It is the American story; from the nation's inception hundreds of years ago and on long into the future, this tale will be told.

As for the practical side of this book, while these drinks are undeniably alluring and delicious, some may need to be taken with a grain of salt, or adjusted to one's palette (for example, one could substitute a liquorice whip for a lolly pop or a hammer for a screwdriver, etc.). If you need to slow down an IRS agent, offer them a Tax Collector or Wily Withholder. For reasons that are still unclear, these drinks are especially effective when used on people in the tax business. They will be loopy for quite awhile so you can make a speedy getaway.

That about wraps it up. Power through your taxes this year, don't forget to have a few drinks, and be audacious when you claim write-offs. Remember, there is a man out there who got a pool deducted because his doctor said he needed to lose weight. Even the craziest idea has merit, as long as it's not writing off the cost of paying an arsonist to commit insurance fraud.

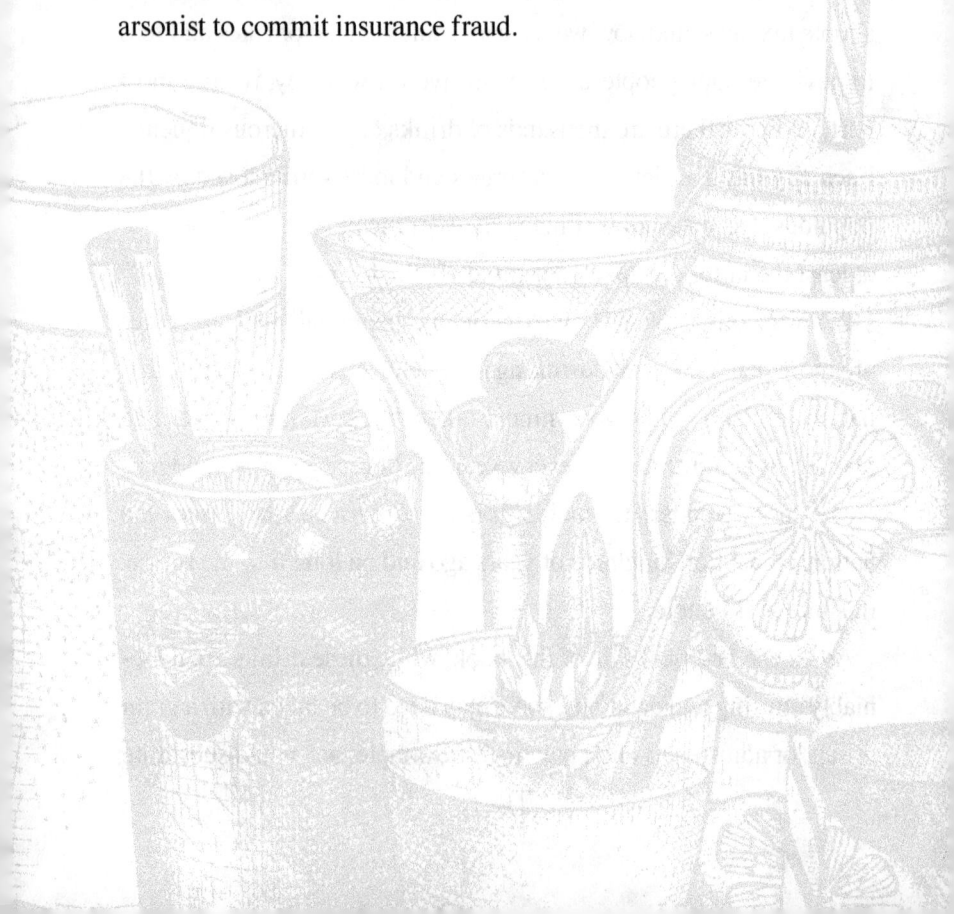

About the Author

Michael Carminucci is a hands-on tax advisor with over thirty years' experience assisting his local community as well as people coast-to-coast. Michael has developed a team of tax specialists who thoroughly inspect a client's income and expenditures to make the tax laws work in their favor. His experience in the industry is vast. He has the designation of enrolled agent, which allows him to prepare more complicated tax returns and offer a wider range of services, perhaps the most important of which is to help his clients with audits and represent them at IRS appeals. Michael's other designations are: RFC (registered financial consultant), CFS (certified fund specialist), and CDFA (certified divorce financial analyst). Mike has also gleaned the helpful impact an occasional drink can have when going through the tax process. After many years of careful research, Michael would like to share some of his concoctions with the world.